TALK ABOUT
VALUES

Conversation Skills for Intermediate Students

Irene E. Schoenberg

Talk About Values

Longman, 10 Bank Street, White Plains, N.Y. 10606

Associated companies:
Longman Group Ltd., London
Longman Cheshire Pty., Melbourne
Longman Paul Pty., Auckland
Copp Clark Pitman, Toronto
Pitman Publishing Inc., New York

Distributed in the United Kingdom by Longman Group Ltd., Longman House, Burnt Mill,
Harlow, Essex CM20 2JE, England, and by associated companies, branches, and
representatives throughout the world.

We would like to thank United Features Syndicate, Inc.
for giving us permission to reprint the cartoon on page 58.

Executive editor: Joanne Dresner
Development editor: Nancy Perry
Design and production: The Quarasan Group, Inc.
Illustrations: Judith DuFour Love, pages 12, 52, 57; Steve McInturff, pages 29, 40; Eileen Mueller-
Neill, pages 7, 24, 28, 34; Bill Petersen, page 63; Arnie Ten, page 1; George Ulrich, pages 19, 37, 38,
46, 50.
Production supervisor: Kathleen M. Ryan

ISBN: 0-8013-0011-8

9 10 - CRS - 98 97 96 95 94

This book is for my parents,
Rita and Paul Steiner,
whose values I admire.

Acknowledgments

I'd like to express my sincere appreciation to my wonderful friends, colleagues and students at the International English Language Institute of Hunter College for helping and advising me with this book. In particular, a very special thanks to Pamela McPartland, director of the International English Language Institute for her genuine interest and invaluable suggestions, to Alison Rice for her perceptive observations and to Robert Fertita and Sonja Rimokh for their many discerning comments at an early stage. In addition, I'd like to thank Peter Thomas, Julie Falsetti, Susan Stempleski, Carole Rosen, Corinne Lyons, James Willimetz, Leila May-Landy and Tracey Forrest for their enthusiasm, encouragement, and recommendations.

My editors, Joanne Dresner and Nancy Perry, provided invaluable help in strengthening the book and working on the fine details. It was truly a pleasure to work with them.

Finally to my loving family I owe my greatest debt: most of all to my husband Harris, who is always there to listen and advise on anything I write; to my parents Rita and Paul Steiner and my father-in-law, Jacques Schoenberg, who always support me; and to my children, Dani and Dahlia, who have given me the chance to talk and talk about values and, perhaps, to pass on some good ones.

Contents

Introduction

- Your neighbor's child is crying because your neighbor is hitting and hurting her.
- Your friend wants to know what you think of the ugly new sweater she bought and can't return.
- You're about to marry a man with no money. You want to keep your bank accounts separate, but he insists on opening a joint account.
- You are late for a job interview when you notice a button missing on your suit.
- Your soccer team has a game this afternoon. Your friend has offered you free tickets to a concert at the same time, and you would love to go.

What do you do? What do you say? Is a neighbor's privacy more important than an individual's safety? Is honesty more important than a friend's feelings? Does marriage mean that you share all you have? Is punctuality more important than appearance at a job interview? Is loyalty to a team more important than personal desires? These and many other questions are raised in **Talk About Values,** a book that stimulates students to communicate because it provokes them to express their personal beliefs and to discuss their own conflicting values. At the same time, it encourages students to compare their values with those of classmates with other personalities and from other cultures and backgrounds. Because there are no correct answers to values questions, students come to realize that no one can be wrong. They lose their fear of failure and concentrate on using English to discuss the issues and convince their classmates.

Talk About Values is for adults and young adults at the intermediate level. It prepares students for values questions with a step-by-step approach that gradually familiarizes them with the subject. Each of the twelve chapters contains at least seven sections that proceed from the more simple and concrete (describe a picture, talk about a short reading, answer personal questions) to the more difficult and abstract (solve a values problem, create a roleplay, discuss a proverb).

Talk About Values is flexible. It contains group work, pair work, work for the entire class and work for the student to do alone. Suggested roleplays with useful functions appear in every chapter, as well as a proverb, joke and suggested writing topics. Teachers may wish to pick and choose the activities that best suit their particular class or go through an entire chapter.

To give students additional practice with the vocabulary used in the text, an appendix contains a fill-in exercise and a crossword puzzle for each chapter. Teachers may wish to use the material in the appendix to preview or to review each chapter.

The richness of each chapter of **Talk About Values** provides hours of stimulating conversation at a level that intermediate students will be able to handle and enjoy.

You and Your Neighbors

1 **Look at the picture and answer the questions.**

1. What's happening in each apartment?
2. Which people are having a good time? Why?
3. Which people are unhappy? Why?

For practice with vocabulary in Chapter 1, see page 72.

2 **Read the paragraph and answer the questions.**

What Is a Good Neighbor?

There are different kinds of neighbors. One neighbor can save your life. Another neighbor can make your life miserable. Some people think a good neighbor should only say hello and ask about the weather. Others think a good neighbor should be a good friend.

1. Have you ever helped a neighbor in trouble or saved a neighbor's life? Explain.
2. Has a neighbor ever helped you or saved your life? Explain.

3 **Think about your experiences. First answer the questions by yourself. Then ask a classmate.**

	You	Your Classmate
1. Do you live in an apartment, a private house or a dormitory?		
2. Are the walls in your home thick or thin?		
3. Do your neighbors: a) have any noisy pets?		
b) practice any instruments?		
c) listen to loud music?		
4. What sounds do you hear when you're at home?		
5. Have you met your neighbors?		

	You	*Your Classmate*
6. Do you know your neighbors: a) very well?		
b) not so well?		
7. Think about a neighbor. Do you know this person's: a) name?		
b) job?		
c) hobbies?		
8. What word or words would you use to describe this person? a) quiet		
b) helpful		
c) considerate		
d) hospitable		
e) friendly		
f) inconsiderate		
g) nosy		
h) noisy		
i) unfriendly		
j) ?		

continued

Now work as a class and answer the questions.

1. Describe your classmate's neighbor. How does this person compare to your neighbor?
2. Do you think neighbors are friendlier in some countries than in others?
3. In your opinion, what is a good neighbor?

4   **In small groups, read about each problem. Then talk about the situation and decide what you would do.**

1. You live next door to a musician. He practices the piano every day from two in the afternoon until midnight. Several times you've asked him not to practice at night. Each time, he stops practicing for two or three nights, but then he starts again. You're getting very angry. You solve the problem by:
a) buying ear plugs.
b) writing a letter to your neighbor.
c) complaining to the police.
d) moving.
e) _____?_____

2. You're in your apartment, and you hear loud crying. You think the woman next door is hitting one of her children and hurting the child. You:
a) mind your own business.
b) bang on the wall.
c) visit the family.
d) call the police.
e) _____?_____

3. You moved to a new home four months ago. The woman next door was very helpful when you moved in. You were grateful and invited her to dinner. Soon she began dropping in right after dinner and staying for about two hours. At first you thought it was nice. Now she visits you every evening, and you don't enjoy her visits. You:
a) pretend not to be home.
b) open the door and tell her you're busy.
c) tell her exactly how you feel.
d) _____?_____

5 **With a partner, read the paragraph. Then write a short conversation with your partner and act it out.**

You are a student. You study best in a quiet room. Your neighbor is an old man. He doesn't hear well but likes to listen to the radio all day long. He has a dog and a bird that wake you up at 5:00 A.M. Sometimes, when he can't sleep at night, he plays his violin.

Use one expression from each box in your conversation.

Complaining	*Apologizing*
The noise from your _____ is really bothering me. Your _____ is so loud I can't _____.	I'm so sorry. I didn't mean to . . . I apologize.

Begin like this:

YOU: I hate to disturb you, but . . .

6 **Explain this expression.**

Good fences make good neighbors.
     —Robert Lee Frost, "Mending Walls"

Are there any expressions about neighbors in your culture?

Now listen as your teacher reads the following joke.

A woman was talking to her next-door neighbor.
"We're going to be living in a better neighborhood soon," she said.
"So are we," her neighbor said.
"What? Are you moving too?"
"No, we're staying here."

Would this joke be funny in your language? Do you know a similar joke?

7 Writing Suggestions

Write about a neighbor you have had or make up a story about a neighbor that fits one of the following descriptions:

1. My Noisy Neighbor
2. My Nosy Neighbor
3. My Unusual Neighbor
4. My Terrible Neighbor
5. My Helpful Neighbor

How Honest Are You?

1 **Look at the pictures and answer the questions.**

1. If you were the friend in the first cartoon, or the young man in the second, what would you have said?

2. Do you think the people in the cartoons were wrong for not being honest?

For practice with vocabulary in Chapter 2, see page 74.

2 **Read the passage and answer the questions.**

Teaching Honesty Is Difficult

We teach young children to be honest. We tell them about great leaders who were very honest. We read stories to them in which bad things happen to dishonest people—noses grow, wolves eat them.*

Yet, as children get older, we tell them the importance and even the benefit of the "white lie." At times it is difficult to decide when to be completely honest and when to tell a small lie.

1. Can you think of any famous people who were known for their honesty?
2. Are there any stories in your culture that teach honesty to children?

3 **Think about your experiences. First answer the questions by yourself. Then ask a classmate.**

	You	Your Classmate
1. Did you ever say you were: a) sick when you were not sick?		
b) older or younger than you were?		
2. If you answered "yes," how did you feel afterwards?		
3. How do you feel when you discover a person has lied to you? a) angry		
b) hurt		
c) sad		

*The stories of *Pinocchio* and *The Boy Who Cried Wolf*

	You	*Your Classmate*
d) ashamed		
e) all of the above		
f) ?		
4. Do you know anyone who: a) took something small from a hotel, airline or restaurant (an ashtray, a towel)?		
b) cheated on a test?		
c) stole a small thing when he or she was a young child?		
5. If you answered ''yes,'' how do you feel about it?		
6. How would you feel if you discovered that someone took something that belonged to you?		

Now work as a class and answer the questions.

1. Did you and your classmate have any similar experiences?
2. In what situations do you think it's OK to tell a white lie?
3. In what situations do you think it's OK to take something that doesn't belong to you or cheat on a test?
4. Is it difficult to teach children to be honest? Why?

4 **In small groups, read about each problem. Then talk about the situation and decide what you would do.**

1. You find an expensive ring in the bathroom of a restaurant. You:
  a) keep it.
  b) give it to the manager of the restaurant.
  c) give it to a friend.
  d) _____?_____

2. You find a dollar in the bathroom of a restaurant. You:
   a) keep it.
   b) leave it in the bathroom.
   c) give it to the manager of the restaurant.
   d) _____?_____

3. Your twelve-year-old son is very happy. He shows you an old comic book. He bought it from a classmate for a dollar. The comic book is worth $50. Your son knew it was valuable, but the other boy didn't. You:
   a) congratulate your son on being a good businessman.
   b) tell your son to sell the comic and share the profit with his friend.
   c) tell your son that he was dishonest and make him return the comic book.
   d) _____?_____

4. You have just eaten in a restaurant. The food and service were terrible. When you pay your bill, the cashier makes a mistake and gives you too much change. You:
   a) return the extra change.
   b) keep the change. After all, you suffered through a terrible meal.
   c) _____?_____

5. You have just returned from the supermarket with a week's worth of groceries. You discover that you have an extra bag of groceries. It's a long walk back to the store. You:
   a) return the extra bag of groceries.
   b) enjoy the extra bag of groceries.
   c) _____?_____

6. Your friend bought a new sweater. She asks what you think of it. You don't like it, but you know that she can't return the sweater. You say:
   a) "It's a beautiful sweater."
   b) "I'm not crazy about the sweater."
   c) "I have to get used to the sweater."
   d) "I don't really like it."
   e) _____?_____

5 **With a partner, read the paragraph. Then write a short conversation with your partner and act it out.**

A co-worker wants to talk about your new boss, but you don't. You like your new boss, but your co-worker doesn't. When he tries to talk about the boss, you disagree and change the subject.

Use one of the expressions below in your conversation:

Changing the subject

Say, did you hear, . . .

By the way, . . .

Begin like this:

CO-WORKER: Isn't our new boss a fool?

YOU: Oh, I don't really think so . . .

6 **Explain this expression.**

Honesty is the best policy.

Are there any expressions about honesty in your culture?

Now listen as your teacher reads the following joke.

A six-year-old boy gets on the bus with his mother. A sign says, "Children five years old or under ride for free." The mother whispers to her son, "If the bus driver wants to know your age, tell him you're five years old." Sure enough, the bus driver asks the boy, "How old are you?" The boy answers, "Five years old." The bus driver looks at the boy and says, "When will you be six?" The boy responds, "As soon as I get off the bus."

Would this joke be funny in your language? Do you know a similar joke?

7 **Writing Suggestions**

Write about one of the following experiences you may have had.

1. a time you told a white lie

2. a time you decided to tell the truth even though it would have been easier to lie

3. a time you were sorry that you either had lied or had told the truth

What Men Look for in a Wife
What Women Look for in a Husband

1 **Look at the pictures and decide which woman you would match with which man. Give one reason for each match.**

1

Dahlia McPartland
Age: 33
Profession: doctor
Income: $85,000
Hobbies: tennis, travel
Personality: quiet, serious, industrious

2

Gabrielle Harris
Age: 27
Profession: artist
Income: $20,000 (average)
Hobbies: cooking, movies, dancing
Personality: outgoing, funny, easygoing, talkative

3

Elizabeth Rice
Age: 26
Profession: police officer
Income: $27,000
Hobbies: listening to music, swimming, target practice
Personality: practical, athletic, neat and clean

a

Jimmy Walters
Age: 27
Profession: writer
Income: $22,000 (average)
Hobbies: movies, reading, travel
Personality: romantic, easygoing, talkative

b

Raymond Lee
Age: 30
Profession: high school teacher
Income: $30,000
Hobbies: carpentry, painting, tennis
Personality: neat and clean, practical, quiet

c

Steve Ledesma
Age: 35
Profession: lawyer
Income: $90,000
Hobbies: tennis, racquetball, soccer
Personality: competitive, talkative, hardworking

For practice with vocabulary in Chapter 3, see page 76.

2 **Read the paragraph and answer the question.**

The Right Choice

A man was going out with a beautiful woman. After a short time, he left her. None of the man's friends could understand why. Not only was the woman beautiful, but she was smart and charming as well. When questioned about leaving her, the man held out his shoe. He explained, "This shoe is very fine. It is well made. It is a beautiful material and color. Yet, none of you knows where it hurts me."

Why did the man compare his girlfriend to his shoe?

3 **Give your opinions. First answer the questions by yourself. Put a check (✓) next to each description in the category you think it belongs.**

Then your teacher will ask how many students chose each category. You will write down the results.

Categories: *A = very important*   *C = slightly important*
                B = important   *D = not important*

		For a husband				For a wife			
		A	B	C	D	A	B	C	D
1. a person who can save money	my answer								
	class results								
2. a person who can make enough money for a family to live well	my answer								
	class results								

continued

		For a husband				For a wife			
		A	B	C	D	A	B	C	D
3. a good cook	my answer								
	class results								
4. a person my parents like	my answer								
	class results								
5. a romantic person	my answer								
	class results								
6. an honest person	my answer								
	class results								
7. a hardworking person	my answer								
	class results								
8. a person who is there when things are bad	my answer								
	class results								

		For a husband				For a wife			
		A	B	C	D	A	B	C	D
9. a person who laughs at the same things I do	my answer								
	class results								
10. a person who loves children	my answer								
	class results								
11. a very attractive person	my answer								
	class results								
12. a quiet, reserved person	my answer								
	class results								
13. a talkative, outgoing person	my answer								
	class results								
14. a person who can keep a home neat and clean	my answer								
	class results								

continued

Now work as a class and answer the questions.

1. What was very important for the largest number of students:
   a) for a husband?
   b) for a wife?
2. Did the entire class agree on any categories? Which ones?
3. Were more items "very important" for a husband or for a wife? Why?
4. Would your parents give different answers for some questions? Which ones?
5. Can you think of another important quality for a husband or wife?
6. Do you think people from different countries look for different qualities?

As a result of your discussion, can you reach any conclusions? Did you learn anything new about your classmates?

4 **In small groups, read about each problem. Then talk about the situation and decide what you would do.**

1. Your friend is thinking about marrying a woman who is unlike him in every way. He's messy; she's neat. He's talkative; she's quiet. He's lazy; she's hardworking. He's a good cook; she can't cook at all. He hates all sports; she's very athletic. He's always cheerful; she rarely smiles. You:
   a) advise your friend not to marry her.
   b) wish your friend lots of luck.
   c) think "opposites attract."
   d) _____?_____

2. Your niece has introduced you to the man she plans to marry. He's twice her age. You:
   a) advise her not to marry him.
   b) wish her luck.
   c) _____?_____

3. Your nephew has introduced you to the woman he plans to marry. She's twice his age. You:
   a) advise him not to marry her.
   b) wish him luck.
   c) _____?_____

4. You and your sweetheart have a wonderful relationship in every way. When you began discussing marriage, you discovered that you disagree in one big way. You want to have many children. Your sweetheart doesn't want any. You:
a) look for a new sweetheart.
b) try to convince your sweetheart to change his or her mind.
c) change your mind.
d) _____?_____

5 **With a partner, read the paragraph. Then write a short conversation with your partner and act it out.**

It's Saturday morning. A husband and wife are trying to make plans for the day. Every time she makes a suggestion (how about taking a walk, going to the movies, visiting friends, painting the bathroom), he rejects it. When he has an idea (watching TV, going to a ball game, visiting his mother), she doesn't like it.

Use the expressions below in your conversation.

Making suggestions	*Accepting a suggestion*
Why don't we (take a walk)?	That's a good idea.
How about (taking a walk)?	OK. Why not?
Let's (take a walk).	

Rejecting suggestions

I don't enjoy (taking a walk).
I'd rather not (take a walk).
I really don't want to (take a walk).

Begin like this:

WIFE: It's such a beautiful day! Why don't we . . .

6 **Explain this expression.**

Keep your eyes open before marriage; half shut afterwards.
  —Benjamin Franklin

Benjamin Franklin lived in the 1700s. Do you think what he wrote is still true today?

Now listen as your teacher reads the following joke.

An unhappily married man went to City Hall to find out when his marriage license expires.

Would this joke be funny in your language? Do you know a similar joke?

7 **Writing Suggestions**

1. Comment on the following:
   Many people marry when they are in their 20s. Yet, people grow, develop and change throughout their lives. No wonder marriage is so difficult.

2. Write on one of these topics:
   a) The Wife's Role in a Marriage Today
   b) The Husband's Role in a Marriage Today

1 **Look at the pictures and answer the questions.**

1. When some people are old, they move to a community with other old people. What are the advantages of living with other people your age? What are the disadvantages?
2. Sometimes old people move in with their children and grandchildren. What are the advantages of this arrangement? What are the disadvantages?
3. Sometimes old people prefer to live apart from their children. Why? What are the advantages of this arrangement? What are the disadvantages?

For practice with vocabulary in Chapter 4, see page 78.

2   **Read the paragraph and answer the questions.**

Too Old to Work Here

Mr. Beckoff was an English teacher. He taught for over forty years. When he was seventy years old, he had to retire. He didn't want to leave, but according to the rule of the school, he had to.

1. What do you think of the rule?
2. Are there special rules about retirement in your native country?

3   **Think about your experiences and give your opinions. First answer the questions by yourself. Then ask a classmate.**

	You	*Your Classmate*
1. At what age do men usually retire in your country?		
2. At what age do women usually retire?		
3. At what age do you want to retire?		
4. When you retire, do you want to live: a) alone?		
b) with your husband or wife?		
c) with your children?		
d) in a community with people your age?		
5. Have you ever known an old person well?		
Did you help that person in any way?		
Did that person teach you anything?		
Did that person have any special problems because of his or her age?		

Now work as a class and answer the questions.

1. Did you and your classmate agree on the best retirement age? On the best place to live when you retire? Explain.
2. In what ways can younger people help old people?
3. What can younger people learn from old people?
4. In your opinion, what are the biggest problems for old people?

4 **In small groups, read about each problem. Then talk about the situation and decide what you would do.**

1. You have a seat on a bus. An old woman gets on the bus. There are no empty seats. You:
   a) give up your seat
   b) ask a child to give up his or her seat.
   c) keep your seat and look the other way.
   d) _____?_____

2. All seats on the bus are taken. You get on the bus at the same time as an old man with a cane. Nobody gives the old man a seat. You:
   a) ask a young person to give the old man his seat.
   b) ask the bus driver to tell someone to get up.
   c) don't say anything out loud, but use your eyes to suggest that someone give the man a seat.
   d) feel sorry for the old man but don't do anything about it.
   e) _____?_____

3. You're standing in line at the supermarket. An old man with a full shopping cart asks to get ahead of you. You:
   a) let him.
   b) don't let him.
   c) _____?_____

4. You live in a small town with few people over sixty-five. The city planners want to build 2,000 apartments for the old. Some say the old people will vote against spending money on schools and parks for children. Others say that old people belong in every community. You are:
   a) in favor of these apartments.
   b) against these apartments.
   c) in favor of some apartments but think there should be fewer.
   d) _____?_____

5 **With a partner, read the paragraph. Then write a short conversation with your partner and act it out.**

Henry and Rosie's son is married and has four children of his own. He and his wife would like Henry and Rosie to move in with them. Henry thinks it's a great idea, but Rosie is totally against it.

Use the expressions below in your conversation:

> *Talking about future obligations*
>
> We'll have to . . .
> We won't have to . . .

Begin like this:

HENRY: I really think we should move in with the children. We'll live together as one big, happy family.
ROSIE: But, Henry, we'll have to change our whole way of living.
HENRY: What do you mean?
ROSIE: We'll have to . . .

6 **Read the story by yourself. Then, as a class, discuss the answers to the questions.**

A Coat for Grandpa

Joe lived with his wife and nine-year-old son in a big house. One day, Joe's eighty-year-old father came to visit. The old man spent the afternoon playing with his grandson, Billy. Before leaving, the grandfather said to his son, "I'm sorry to bother you, but I'm a little worried. Winter is coming, and my apartment is so cold. And winter is so long."

Joe looked annoyed and said, "Oh, father. You know I would like to help you, but with the new house and the car, I can't. Maybe next year I'll be able to help you."

The grandfather quickly answered, "Oh, I understand."

The old man was about to leave when Joe turned to young Billy and said, "Billy, run upstairs and bring down that old winter coat for Grandpa."

Billy ran upstairs and came down with the coat. He looked at his father and then at his grandfather. He tore the coat in two. Joe shouted, "Billy! What's wrong with you? Why did you tear that coat in two?"

The child looked at his father and quietly said, "Oh, Daddy. I'm saving the other half for you."

1. Why do you think Billy tore the coat in two? Was he angry at his father? Did he think he was being helpful?

2. How do you think the father felt at the end of this story?

7 **Explain this expression.**

One mother can take care of six children, but six children cannot take care of one mother.

Are there any expressions about old people in your culture?

8 **Writing Suggestions**

1. Describe one of your grandparents or any older person that you have known and cared about.

2. Try to describe how you expect to live when you are seventy years old.

Borrowing and Lending

from   to

1 **Look at the pictures and answer the questions.**

1

2

3

1. How do the father, the co-workers and the friend seem to feel about lending something?

2. What are the advantages and disadvantages of lending or borrowing things?

For practice with vocabulary in Chapter 5, see page 80.

2   **Read the paragraph and answer the question.**

A Really Great Guy

All of Joe's friends say he's a wonderful guy. When a friend needs money, Joe is ready to lend it. When a friend needs a favor, Joe is there to do it. When a friend needs a ride, Joe offers to take him. When Joe and his friends go to a restaurant, Joe usually pays the bill. Everyone loves Joe. Everyone thinks Joe is great. Everyone, except Joe's wife. She thinks he's too generous.

Can a person be too generous? How?

3   **Think about your experiences and give your opinions. First answer the question by yourself. Then ask a classmate.**

Which statement is true about you?

	You	*Your Classmate*
1. I try never to borrow or lend money. I never like to ask friends or relatives for money. If I have to borrow money, I prefer going to a bank.		
2. I don't like to borrow or lend money. If I really need to, I reluctantly ask my family or close friends.		
3. I feel good about lending money to friends and relatives who need it. If I need some money, I feel good about asking my friends or relatives.		
4. I feel good about lending to friends or relatives. I hate to borrow money from anyone.		

continued

Now work as a class and answer the questions.

1. Do you and your classmates have the same attitude about borrowing and lending money?

2. How many students checked 1?   2?   3?   4?

3. Do you think that borrowing or lending money among friends and relatives is more common in some cultures than in others? Explain.

4   **In small groups, read about each problem. Then talk about the situation and decide what you would do.**

1. A co-worker asks to borrow $30. You don't know her very well. You:
   a) lend her the money and hope to get it back.
   b) lend her the money but ask for a receipt.
   c) make an excuse.
   d) _____?_____

2. A good friend owes you $100. He promised to pay you back two months ago. You reminded him about it twice in the past three weeks. Now you:
   a) forget about the money. Your friendship is worth more than $100.
   b) speak to him again.
   c) send him a letter from your lawyer.
   d) _____?_____

3. You got married a few months ago. You and your spouse both work far from your home. You each take two buses and a train to get to work. Your in-laws rarely use their car. They want to lend it to you. Your spouse wants to use it, but you don't. You:
   a) borrow their car to please your spouse.
   b) tell your spouse to use the car, but you continue to take the buses and train.
   c) don't borrow their car. Everyone will feel terrible if something happens to it.
   d) _____?_____

5   **With a partner, read the paragraph. Then write a short conversation with your partner and act it out.**

   You and your roommate will be out of town for three weeks. Your friend Oscar has recently separated from his wife. He asked if he could stay in your house for the three weeks that you are away. You would like to let him stay because he is your friend. However, your roommate is very much against it because Oscar always invited friends to his home and his home was always a mess. Your roommate is afraid Oscar or one of his friends will destroy your house.

Use one expression from each box in your conversation.

Expressing an opinion

In my opinion, Oscar should stay in our home.
I think Oscar will ruin our beautiful furniture.

Disagreeing

I disagree. I think it's good to have someone in the house while we are away.
I don't think so. Oscar will take good care of our plants and fish.

Begin like this:

YOU: I don't think Oscar should stay at our house . . .

---

6 **Read the story by yourself. Then, as a class, discuss the answers to the questions.**

All in the Family

Thirty years ago, Carmen and her husband arrived in a new country and wanted to open a small grocery store. They didn't have enough money, so Carmen went to her brother, Luis, and asked to borrow some money.

He agreed to lend Carmen the money but said, "I have my money in the bank, and I'm getting interest on it. I will lend you the money if you pay me the same rate of interest as the bank."

Carmen took the money and paid it back with interest. She never spoke about it, but she could never forget that her brother had charged her interest.

1. In your opinion, was Luis right or wrong?
2. Was Carmen right or wrong?
3. How would you have acted?

7 **Explain this expression.**

Neither a borrower nor a lender be.
    —William Shakespeare

Are there are any expressions about borrowing or lending in your culture?

Now listen as your teacher reads the following joke.

Ron's neighbor asked to borrow his hammer.
"Sorry," said Ron. "I have to shave."
When the neighbor left, Ron's wife said, "Why did you give such a silly excuse?"
Ron replied, "If you don't want to do a thing, one excuse is as good as another."

Would this joke be funny in your language? Do you know a similar joke?

8 **Write an answer to the following letter.**

Dear _____,

    How have you been? Susan and I are both fine. We have been working hard and are looking forward to our vacation. We're hoping to spend some time in your city next July. We met Derek Howards last week, and he mentioned that you're planning to be out of town in July. Susan and I were wondering if we could use your apartment for about two **weeks** - from July 1 through July 15. Anytime you're in our city, you're welcome to stay with us.

    We'll understand if you say no, but we hope you'll say yes. Hope to hear from you soon.

        Fondly,

        _____

Red Faces

1 **Look at the pictures and answer the questions.**

Have you ever had experiences like those of the people in the pictures?
What happened?

For practice with vocabulary in Chapter 6, see page 82.

2 **Read the passage and answer the question.**

Oops! I Made a Mistake

"When I realized what I had said, I wanted to dig a hole in the ground and disappear."

Most of us can remember a time when we "put our foot in our mouth." Generally, this happens when we speak without thinking first. But sometimes it happens when we speak to someone from a different culture. Such simple things as calling a person by his or her first name or asking a person his or her age or weight can be very embarrassing if it's the wrong time, place or person.

In English, when you say the wrong thing, we say you "put your foot in your mouth." Is there a similar expression in your native language?

3 **Think about your experiences and give your opinions. First answer the question by yourself. Then ask a classmate.**

Are these questions acceptable, a little impolite *or very* impolite?

	You	*Your Classmate*
1. You are middle-aged. A classmate asks, "How old are you?"		
2. You are in your twenties. A classmate asks, "How old are you?"		
3. You gained a lot of weight in the last year. Your mother-in-law asks, "How much did you gain?"		
4. You are average weight. A classmate asks, "How much do you weigh?"		

	You	*Your Classmate*
5. Your best friend asks, "How much money do you make?"		
6. You meet someone for the first time. The person asks, "How much money do you make?"		
7. You are over twenty-five. A co-worker asks, "Why aren't you married?"		
8. A co-worker asks, "Who did you vote for?"		
9. *Now write your own impolite question.*		

Now work as a class and answer the questions.

1. Did you and your classmate agree on which questions were impolite and which were acceptable?

2. What makes a question impolite?

3. Are there any questions that are acceptable in some cultures that are not polite in others? Explain.

4. Read the impolite question you wrote in #9 to the class. Is this question polite to ask in any culture?

4 **In small groups, read about each problem. Then talk about the situation and decide what you would do.**

1. You and two co-workers work part time in a store. Your boss gave you a raise last month but said, "I want to give you more money than your co-workers because you work harder. But please don't tell the others." Yesterday one of your co-workers asked, "How much money are you making? I'm getting $5 an hour. Are you getting more?" You answer:
   a) "Yes, I'm getting $6 an hour, but please don't tell anyone."
   b) "I'm earning about the same as you."
   c) "None of your business."
   d) "No."
   e) _____?_____

2. You meet a friend you haven't seen for a few months. You ask, "How's your husband?" She says, "We got divorced two months ago." You say:
a) "I'm really sorry to hear that."
b) "Good for you. I never liked him."
c) "Why?"
d) _____?_____

3. Two years ago, your favorite nephew became the director of a big company in a far-away city. Upon arriving in your city on business, he invites you to dinner. When you see him, you are shocked. He looks ten years older. He has gained at least thirty pounds. He smokes at least twenty cigarettes during dinner. You:
a) never say anything about his appearance.
b) wait for him to say something about his appearance.
c) make a joke about how he looks.
d) tell him he looks terrible.
e) _____?_____

5   **With a partner, read the paragraph. Then write a short conversation with your partner and act it out.**

You see someone. You're sure that you know that person. You greet him or her and discover that you made a mistake.

Use one expression from each box in your conversation.

Confirming information
Aren't you the man who delivers the newspapers?
You're the man who delivers the newspapers, **aren't you?**
Don't you work in the supermarket?
You work in the supermarket, **don't you?**
Weren't you my teacher in the seventh grade?
You were my teacher in the seventh grade, **weren't you?**

Contradicting someone

I'm afraid you're mistaken. I'm not . . .
You must be mistaken. I don't . . .
I don't think so. I wasn't . . .

Begin like this:

YOU: Aren't you . . .

Now change partners and act out another conversation.

6   **Explain this expression.**

Man is the only animal that blushes. Or needs to.
    —Mark Twain

Are there any expressions about being embarrassed in your culture?

Now listen as your teacher reads the following joke.

> A kindergarten teacher smiled at the man opposite her on
> the bus. He didn't answer. Realizing her mistake, she said
> aloud, "Oh, please excuse mc. I made a mistake. I thought you
> were the father of one of my children." She got off at the next
> stop.
>
>   *—The Wall Street Journal*

Would this joke be funny in your language? Do you know a similar joke?

7   **Writing Suggestion**

Write about a time that you or someone you knew made a mistake and felt
embarrassed. Explain why you felt embarrassed.

Dress for Success

1 **Look at the picture and answer the questions.**

1. Why are the people in the picture upset?
2. Have you ever had an experience like that of the people in the picture? What happened?

For practice with vocabulary in Chapter 7, see page 84.

2 **Read the passage and answer the question.**

Appearances

Even before we open our mouths, people look at us and form an opinion about us. That's why most people feel good when they look good.

Sometimes, however, we become too concerned with how we look or how others look to us. Then we forget that a beautifully wrapped package may have nothing inside.

What do you think a person's clothes tell us about the person?

3 **Think about your experiences and give your opinions. First answer the questions by yourself. Then ask a classmate.**

	You	Your Classmate
1. When you shop for clothes what is most important for you: a) the color?		
b) the style?		
c) the comfort?		
d) the price?		
e) how it looks on you?		
2. What is least important for you?		
3. Do you think what you wear: a) is important everywhere?		
b) is important only at work?		
c) is not important anywhere? Explain.		

continued

	You	Your Classmate
4. Can the following clothes hurt you? a) old clothes		
b) dirty clothes		
c) very modern clothes		
d) very conservative clothes		
e) torn clothes		
f) tight clothes		
5. Can the wrong clothes prevent a person from getting a job? Explain.		

Now work as a class and answer the questions.

1. Do you and your classmate have the same ideas about clothes?

2. In what ways can clothes help you or hurt you?

4 **In small groups, read about each problem. Then talk about the situation and decide what you would do.**

1. You are late for a job interview. You notice a button is missing on your suit. You:
a) sew on the button.
b) change clothes.
c) go without the button.
d) _____?_____

2. You are at a party. Someone is wearing exactly the same outfit. You:
a) avoid that person.
b) leave the party immediately.
c) say to that person, "You have good taste. I like your outfit."
d) ask that person, "Where did you buy your outfit? How much did you pay?"
e) _____?_____

3. You are the principal of a high school. You:
   a) allow the students to wear whatever they want.
   b) allow the students to wear whatever they want as long as it is neat and clean.
   c) have the students wear uniforms.
   d) _____?_____

5 **Clothes with a message. Answer the questions with a partner.**

Do you or your partner have any T-shirts with writing on them? What do they say?

Have you ever seen these T-shirts?

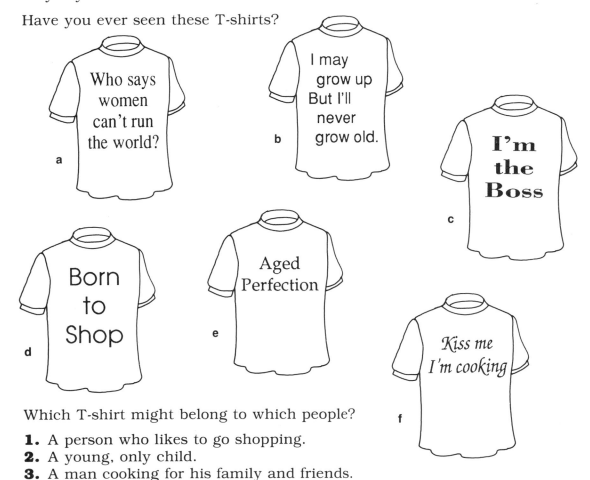

Which T-shirt might belong to which people?

1. A person who likes to go shopping.
2. A young, only child.
3. A man cooking for his family and friends.
4. A woman who has a very important job.
5. An older man who is in good shape.
6. An older woman who feels young.

Now complete the following T-shirts.

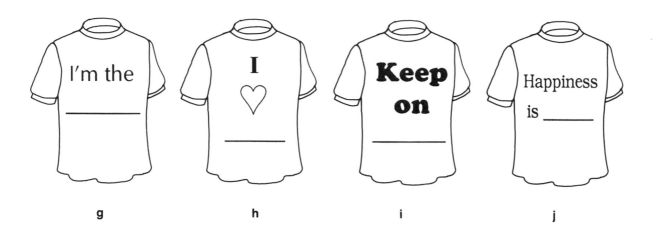

g   h   i   j

Here are some suggestions:

greatest	chocolate	smiling	good friends
best	New York	laughing	speaking English
	my teddy bear	trying	a full stomach

Now write your own T-shirt slogan.

6 **With a partner, read the paragraph. Then write a short conversation with your partner and act it out.**

You and your husband are in a men's store. Your husband needs a suit. He likes a light blue, polyester suit. It is very cheap. You like a dark blue, wool suit. It is very expensive.

Use the following expressions in your conversation.

> *Explaining a choice*
>
> **If I get** the polyester suit, **I'll be able to wash** it in the machine.
> **If you buy** the dark blue suit, **it won't show** the dirt.

Begin like this:

WIFE: Look at this suit. Isn't it beautiful? If you get this suit, . . .

7 **Explain these expressions.**

We say:
    You can't judge a book by its cover.
What does that mean?

We also say:
    Clothes make the man.
What does that mean?

Do you have any expressions about clothes in your culture?

8 **Writing Suggestion**

Describe a man and a woman wearing the very latest styles. You might want to look at a magazine and describe someone in it.

Giving the Right Gift

1 **Look at the pictures and answer the questions.**

1

2

1. What is happening in the pictures?
2. How are the people in each picture related to each other?
3. How do the people feel about their gifts?

For practice with vocabulary in Chapter 8, see page 86.

2 **Read the passage and answer the questions.**

Choosing a Gift

Rita planned to buy her nephew Daniel a tennis racket for his twelfth birthday. But, when Daniel hinted that he really wanted a video game, Rita was uncertain what to get. Rita never liked video games, and Daniel already had two of them.

After considering the two gifts, Rita bought Daniel the tennis racket.

1. Which gift would you have given?
2. Did you consider Daniel's age when you made your decision? If Daniel was going to be eight, would you have made the same choice? What if Daniel was going to be twenty?
3. Have you ever bought a gift that you didn't like but that you thought would please the person you bought it for? What was it? What happened?

3 **Think about your experiences. First answer the questions by yourself. Then ask a classmate.**

	You	*Your Classmate*
1. Approximately how many gifts do you buy in a year? a) less than five		
b) between five and ten		
c) between ten and thirty		
d) more than thirty		

continued

	You	Your Classmate
2. On what occasions? a) birthdays		
b) anniversaries		
c) weddings		
d) graduations		
e) religious holidays		
f) _____?_____		

	You		Your Classmate	
3. For whom? a) family				
b) friends				
c) people who do things for you during the year (e.g., the mail carrier)				

4. Look at the following list. Which gifts do you like to give? Which do you like to receive?	Give	Receive	Give	Receive
a) books				
b) clothes				
c) tickets for concerts, plays or sports events				
d) games				
e) sports equipment				
f) small leather items (e.g., wallets, belts)				
g) toys				

	You		Your Classmate	
	Give	*Receive*	*Give*	*Receive*
h) jewelry				
i) money				
j) flowers or chocolates				
k) handmade gifts				
l) _____?_____				

Now work as a class and answer the questions.

1. Do you and your classmate give gifts on the same occasions?

2. Do you and your classmate like to give and receive the same kinds of gifts?

3. In your opinion, what makes a gift special?

4 **In small groups, read about each problem. Then talk about the situation and decide what you would do.**

1. Two girlfriends invite you to their weddings. One wedding will be a big, formal affair. It will cost a lot of money. The other wedding will be a simple, inexpensive party. You are equally close to both friends. Both families are neither rich nor poor. When it comes to the gift, you:
   a) give both friends gifts that cost the same.
   b) give the friend who is having the more expensive wedding a more expensive gift.
   c) _____?_____

2. You and your cousin have been giving each other birthday gifts for many years. You both recently married. You're now much richer than your cousin. You:
   a) buy her a gift that isn't too expensive because you don't want her to feel she has to buy you an expensive gift.
   b) buy her a very expensive gift because you can afford it and want her to have it.
   c) _____?_____

continued

3. For four years in a row, a friend has given you a bottle of cologne. It's always the same cologne, and you don't like the scent. You have always thanked your friend for the gift, and so, your friend has no idea that you don't really like it. It's coming to that time of year again. You:

a) accept another bottle of cologne.
b) tell your friend that you're allergic to it.
c) tell your friend that you prefer another cologne.
d) _____?_____

5 **In small groups, choose a special gift for the following three people. After your group has decided on the gifts, compare your suggestions with those of the other groups in your class.**

	Your Group's Gift
1. An eleven-year-old boy is graduating from elementary school. His parents are busy doctors. The child has many toys and clothes. He's an only child and spends a lot of time by himself.	
2. A foreign student is going to celebrate her twenty-first birthday next week. She arrived here three months ago. She doesn't have much money or know many people.	
3. A very poor, old couple are celebrating their forty-eighth anniversary. They have few friends, almost no relatives and very little money.	

6 **With a partner, read the paragraph. Then write a short conversation with your partner and act it out.**

A customer asks a salesperson for help in finding a funny present (e.g., a pet rock, sneezing powder, a gold back scratcher) for a friend's surprise thirtieth birthday party. Every time the salesperson makes a suggestion, the customer rejects it.

Use the following expressions in your conversation.

> ### Rejecting suggestions
>
> It's much **too** (expensive, silly, big, heavy).
> It isn't _____ (original, cheap, funny) **enough.**

Begin like this:

SALESPERSON: Can I help you?
CUSTOMER: I hope so. I'm trying to find a funny gift for a friend.
SALESPERSON: Have you seen our . . .

7 Explain this expression.

Give a man a fish
And you feed him for a day.
Teach a man to fish
And you feed him for life.

Can you think of an example that helps explain this expression?

Now listen as your teacher reads the following story.

An Embarrassing Gift

One Saturday night I invited a few friends to my home. It was the first time Andrea and Scott Russell visited me, and they brought a small gift. I thanked them, but I didn't open the gift at the time.

At about midnight, the Russells were getting ready to leave. As they were putting on their coats, I noticed the gift they had brought. I decided to open it. As I opened the gift, Andrea and I both saw a small card inside. The card began, "Dear Andrea and Scott." Without a word, Andrea grabbed the card and put it in her pocket. When we said goodbye, Andrea's face was bright red.

Have you ever received a gift that you didn't want and then given it to someone?

8 Writing Suggestion

Write a composition about a gift you will never forget.

Sports

1 **Look at the pictures and answer the question.**

Is it a good idea to mix teams—young and old, male and female, athletic and unathletic?

For practice with vocabulary in Chapter 9, see page 88.

2 **Read the passage and answer the questions.**

Little League All-Star Players

Little League soccer coach Paul Steiner had to choose three all-star players. Every child on the team wanted to be selected. The first two all-star players were easy to choose. They were by far the best on the team. But the third player was difficult to select. Paul narrowed it down to three players.

The first was Janet Stram, the only girl on the team. She could run fast but wasn't as strong as the others. She enjoyed soccer but missed two games to attend birthday parties.

The second was Marc Williams. He was taller, heavier and stronger than the other two. He had a powerful kick. Sometimes, however, Marc made fun of the poorer players. He missed one game because he was sick.

The third player was Evan Daniels. He was much thinner and shorter than Marc. He was a very good team player, but he couldn't kick as well as Marc. He was quiet, tried hard and never made fun of poorer players.

After considering the choices, Paul finally chose Evan Daniels as the third all-star player.

1. Would you have made the same choice as Paul? Why or why not?
2. Were you ever on a Little League team? Did you enjoy the experience?

3 **Think about your experiences and give your opinions. First answer the questions by yourself. Then ask a classmate.**

	You	*Your Classmate*
1. What's the most popular sport in your country?		
2. What's your favorite sport?		
3. Is keeping score very important for you, or do you prefer playing without keeping score?		

continued

	You	*Your Classmate*
4. Why do you play sports? Rank your answers 1, 2 and 3. a) To win.		
b) To get exercise.		
c) To have fun and relax.		

Now work as a class and answer the questions.

1. Do you and your classmate play sports for the same reasons?

2. What are the different reasons people play sports?

4   **In small groups, read about each problem. Then talk about the situation and decide what you would do.**

1. A girl wants to join the boys' high school basketball team. There is no girls' team. You're the coach of the team. You:
   a) let her join if she's good enough.
   b) don't let her join because you're afraid she may get hurt.
   c) _____?_____

2. A boy wants to join the all-girls' tennis team. He didn't make the boys' team. You're the coach of the girls' team. You:
   a) let him join if he's good enough.
   b) don't let him join because you think it's unfair to the girls on the other teams.
   c) _____?_____

3. You're on a soccer team. The team plays games every week. Your friend invited you to a concert which you would love to go to, but the concert is at the same time as your soccer game. You want to go to the concert, but you don't want to let your team down. You finally decide to:
   a) miss the concert.
   b) miss the soccer game.
   c) _____?_____

4. Your ten-year-old son is a little overweight and not good at sports. He's bright and enjoys art and music. However, in your neighborhood, almost every boy joins the baseball and soccer leagues. Last year he was alone on weekends because all his friends were busy with soccer and baseball. This year you:

    a) tell him to join a sports team. The exercise is good for him, and he may improve. If he's on a winning team, he'll enjoy the game even if he isn't a good player.

    b) tell him not to join a sports team. Children can be mean, and he'll feel hurt.

    c) _____?_____

5. Your fourteen-year-old nephew loves sports. He's a bright boy but a poor student. Last year he was a star player on the basketball team, but his school grades were terrible. This year he wants to join the team again. His mother thinks he should study more and forget about basketball. His father thinks he should be allowed to join the team but get extra help with his schoolwork. They asked for your opinion. You:

    a) agree with his mother.

    b) agree with his father.

    c) _____?_____

5 **With a partner, read the paragraph. Then write a short conversation with your partner and act it out.**

You tell a classmate that you're going to play a game after work (or after school or next weekend). Your classmate asks if you're a good player.

Use the following expressions in your conversation.

> *Describing your abilities*
>
> **I'm not so good at** serving, **but I have a** strong forehand. *(tennis)*
> **I'm good at** catching, **but I'm terrible at** hitting. *(baseball)*
> **I have a strong** kick, **but I'm not so good at** dribbling the ball. *(soccer)*

Begin like this:

        YOU: I'm going to play _____ after work tonight.
CLASSMATE: Oh, are you a good player?

6 **Explain this expression.**

The only bad part of being a good sport is that you have to lose to prove it.
        —Walter Winchell

Are there any expressions about sports in your culture?

Now listen as your teacher reads the following joke.

A: Why is it hot after a baseball game?
B: All the fans go home.

Would this joke be funny in your language? Do you know a similar joke?

7 **Just for Fun. Look at each picture below. Then write the name of the sport it illustrates.**

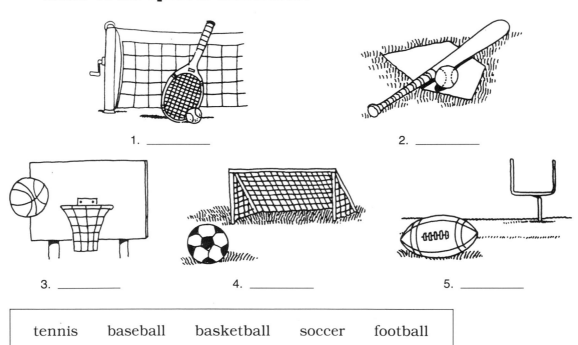

1. _____   2. _____

3. _____   4. _____   5. _____

| tennis   baseball   basketball   soccer   football |

Now write the name of the sport next to the words that are used in that sport.

1. He hit a home run.   _____
2. She got two goals.   _____
3. The score is forty–love.   _____
4. He almost made a basket.   _____
5. It's a touchdown!   _____

8   **Writing Suggestions**

1. Write about your favorite sport. Include the following information:
  a) What do you need to play this sport?
  b) How many people are needed?
  c) How does a person or team win?
  d) When did you first start playing the sport?
  e) Why do you enjoy it?

2. Describe a sports event that you saw. It could be a game in a park, on TV or at a sports stadium or arena.

Pets

1 **Look at the picture and answer the questions.**

What are some of the reasons that people have pets?

For practice with vocabulary in Chapter 10, see page 90.

2 **Read the paragraphs and answer the questions.**

Two Points of View

Terrific Laddie

Every day when you return home after a hard day at work, he is there. He comes to you and sits beside you. He greets you. He's excited to see you. You take a short walk together. Sometimes you play ball. His dinner is simple. You just open a can. He never complains. No wonder you love your dog, Laddie, so much!

Terrible Laddie

Every day when you return home, he has left a mess on your front walk. Some days he eats your flowers, and other days he digs a hole in your garden. Saturday and Sunday he wakes you up at 6:00 A.M. He always rushes up to you and gives you a big, wet kiss when you are wearing your nicest clothes. No wonder you hate your neighbor's dog, Laddie, so much!

1. Have you ever known a terrific dog? What special things did it do?
2. Have you ever known a terrible dog? What awful things did it do?

3 **Think about your experiences and give your opinions. First answer the questions by yourself. Then ask a classmate.**

	You	*Your Classmate*
1. What's the most popular pet in your country?		
2. Have you ever had a pet? If you had a pet: a) Did you enjoy owning it?		
b) What kind was it?		
c) Did you give it a name?		

continued

	You	Your Classmate
d) Did you buy it special food?		
e) Did you buy it special clothes?		
f) Did you talk to it?		
g) Did you teach it to do anything special?		
If you never had a pet: Did you ever want one? Why or why not?		
3. Do you think it's good for children to have pets?		
4. Do you think it's good for old people to have pets?		

Now work as a class and answer the questions.

1. Do you and your classmate feel the same way about having a pet?
2. In your opinion, what are the advantages and disadvantages of owning a pet?

4 **In small groups, read about each problem. Then talk about the situation and decide what you would do.**

1. You need an apartment, but good ones are very difficult to find in the city you are in. You find a wonderful apartment, but pets are not allowed. You have had your cat for five years and don't want to give her away. You:
   a) take the apartment and give your cat to a friend.
   b) take the apartment, keep your cat and hope that nobody will complain.
   c) look for an apartment that allows pets.
   d) _____?_____

2. You live in a private house. Your next-door neighbor's dog comes on your lawn and eats your flowers. You have complained to your neighbor several times. Your neighbor hasn't done anything. You:
a) build a high fence.
b) call the police.
c) have your lawyer write a letter.
d) _____?_____

3. Your sweetheart has a big, ugly, mean dog that you can't stand. You and your sweetheart are in love. You've been talking about marriage, but your sweetheart wants to keep the dog. You:
a) find a new sweetheart.
b) hope to live longer than the dog.
c) learn to love the dog.
d) _____?_____

4. Your children, who are eight and ten years old, want a dog very much. You get them a dog. However, you agree to keep the dog only as long as you don't have anything to do with it. At first, they take good care of the dog. But after three months, they feed and walk the dog only after you have reminded them several times. You:
a) keep on reminding them. After all, they're only children.
b) give the dog away. They must learn to keep their promises.
c) _____?_____

5. A drug company has hired scientists to try and find a cure for a disease. The scientists are doing experiments on monkeys. A group of citizens are protesting. They say the scientists are hurting and killing the monkeys as a result of these experiments, and they want them to stop. The drug company says this is the best way to find a cure for the disease. You are:
a) in favor of the experiments.
b) against the experiments.
c) _____?_____

5 **With a partner, read the paragraph. Then write a short conversation with your partner and act it out.**

A child and his parents are walking by a pet store. The child asks for a pet. The parent explains the work involved. The child says he doesn't mind.

Use the following expressions in your conversation.

Persuading

I don't mind (walking the dog in the rain, cleaning the bird's cage, feeding the cat).
It won't bother me to (walk the dog in the rain, clean the bird's cage, feed the cat).
(Walking the dog in the rain, Cleaning the bird's cage, Feeding the cat) **is not so bad.**

Begin like this:

CHILD: Oh, look at that _____ (adorable, cute, funny, beautiful) _____ (dog, cat, bird, fish, hamster, rabbit). Couldn't we get one?
PARENT: A _____ is a lot of work. You have to _____.
CHILD: I don't mind _____.

6 **Explain this expression.**

A dog is man's best friend.

Are there any expressions about animals in your culture?

Now listen as your teacher reads the following joke.

A young actor tried very hard to please his rich, old aunt by being extremely nice to her dogs. When she died, she remembered her nephew in her will. She left him her three dogs.

Would this joke be funny in your language? Do you know a similar joke?

7   **Just for Fun. Match the animal with its picture.**

| mule | owl | fish | mouse | bird | pig |

1. _____   2. _____   3. _____

4. _____   5. _____   6. _____

Now complete each sentence. Choose from the words above.

1. She never says a word. She's as quiet as a _____.
2. What a messy eater! He eats like a _____.
3. He's a big drinker. He drinks like a _____.
4. He'll never change his mind. He's as stubborn as a _____.
5. She hardly eats at all. She eats like a _____.
6. He always gives good advice. He's as wise as an _____.

8   **Writing Suggestions**

1. Describe a pet you have had.
  a) What was its name?
  b) What did it look like?
  c) Did it have a personality? Describe it.
  d) Is it alive today? How old is it?

2. Look at an animal and describe it. Imagine that it's thinking about something as you're watching it. Write about its thoughts.

UNIT ELEVEN
No Smoking Allowed

1 **Look at the picture and answer the questions.**

1. When you go to a restaurant, are you ever asked if you want to sit in a non-smoking section?
2. If you had a restaurant, where would you seat the smokers?

For practice with vocabulary in Chapter 11, see page 92.

2 **Read the paragraph and answer the question.**

Doctor Refuses Patients Who Smoke

John J. Cannell's father smoked a lot. When John was six years old, his father died of lung cancer. Now John Cannell is a doctor. He is thirty-nine years old. He still remembers his father's terrible death. As a result, he put an advertisement in his local newspaper. It said that Dr. Cannell does not want to care for any new patients who smoke. He says those people should look for another doctor.

—Adapted from *The New York Times,* Feb. 9, 1988

Dr. Cannell will care for patients who are overweight or alcoholics but not for smokers. Some people believe he is "playing God." They believe a doctor should treat anyone who comes to him or her. Do you agree?

3 **Think about your experiences and give your opinions. First answer the questions by yourself. Then ask a classmate.**

	You	*Your Classmate*
1. Do your parents smoke?		
2. Do you smoke? If you do, how many cigarettes do you smoke a day?		
3. If you smoke, when did you first start?		
4. Do you know anyone who gave up smoking? If you do, why did that person stop?		
5. Does it bother you if someone smokes? If it does, do you ask the person to stop smoking?		

continued

	You	*Your Classmate*
6. Are you in favor of "no smoking" rules in the following places? a) restaurants		
b) trains		
c) elevators		
d) hospitals		
e) outdoor stadiums		
f) parks		

Now work as a class and answer the questions.

1. Do you and your classmate agree on having "no smoking" rules in the same places?

2. Why do you think most people stop smoking?

4 **In small groups, read about each problem. Then talk about the situation and decide what you would do.**

1. You are at a company party. There are forty people in one large room. Your supervisor and a few other people are smoking. The smoke is bothering you a lot. You:
   a) force yourself to stay and hide your discomfort.
   b) say something to the people who are smoking.
   c) leave the party.
   d) _____?_____

2. Your uncle is in his seventies. He has always smoked a lot. He seems to be healthy, but you're worried about him. You:
   a) tell him to stop smoking.
   b) don't say anything to him about his smoking.
   c) _____?_____

3. Hunter College in New York City is a "smoke-free" area. This means that people cannot smoke anywhere in the college except for a few special areas. A non-smoking professor wrote an article protesting this new rule. He said that even though he hates the smell of smoke, he believes this rule could lead to rules against other bad habits. For example, people using the Hunter College cafeteria may be forced to eat only healthy foods. Or people working at Hunter College may be forced to do exercise before work. He thinks people have the right to have bad habits. Do you:

    a) agree with this professor?
    b) disagree with this professor?
    c) _____?_____

4. You notice your neighbor's thirteen-year-old son smoking with a group of thirteen year olds. You:

    a) go to him and tell him to stop smoking.
    b) tell his mother that you saw him smoking.
    c) mind your own business.
    d) _____?_____

5 **With a partner, read the paragraph. Then write a short conversation with your partner and act it out.**

You are at a meeting in a small room. One of the people is smoking, and the smoke is bothering you. You ask this person to stop smoking. He or she apologizes.

Use one of the following expressions in your conversation.

Politely asking someone not to do something

Do you mind not smoking? The smoke really bothers me.
Please don't smoke. I can't take the smoke in such a small room.

Begin like this:

YOU *(coughing):*   Do . . .

Now change partners and act out another conversation.

6 Explain this expression.

A sign in a hotel room: "Don't smoke in bed. The ashes that fall on the floor may be your own."

Are there any expressions about bad habits in your culture?

Now listen as your teacher reads the following joke.

Two friends meet. One asks the other for a cigarette. When the man gives his friend the cigarette, he says, "I thought you stopped smoking."

"Well," says the other. "I've only reached the first step. I've stopped buying cigarettes.

Would this joke be funny in your language? Do you know a similar joke?

7 Writing Suggestions

1. Write two paragraphs in which you try to convince teenagers not to smoke.
2. Write about a bad habit that you once had and gave up.

Money

1 **Look at the picture and answer the question.**

"Material Girl" was a popular song in 1985. Do you think that young people today are more interested in money and things that cost money than young people were twenty years ago?

For practice with vocabulary in Chapter 12, see page 94.

2 **Read the passage and answer the question.**

It Pays to Go to School

Red Bank High School in New Jersey is like many other schools in the United States. Most students graduate. However, every year a growing number of students drop out of school before graduation. In order to encourage these students to stay in school, the school is paying them five dollars a day. To receive the money, the students must attend class five days in a row, come to school on time, do all their homework and bring all necessary school supplies. To be in the program, students must have had problems in school in the past.

Some people believe that receiving money will help keep these students in school. Others believe that it is unfair to the majority of students who have never had problems and so are not a part of the program.

—Adapted from *The New York Times,*
March 10, 1988

Do you think paying students to go to school is a good idea?

3 **Think about your experiences and give your opinions. First answer the questions by yourself. Then ask a classmate.**

	You	*Your Classmate*
1. As a child, did you receive an allowance? What did you spend it on?		
2. When did you first earn money? How?		
3. What's more important for you in choosing a job: a) the kind of work?		
b) the salary?		

	You	*Your Classmate*
4. What would be the biggest change in your life if you won a $3 million lottery?		
5. What would be the biggest change in your life if you lost all your money?		

Now work as a class and answer the questions.

1. Would you and your classmate choose a job for the same reasons?

2. Would you and your classmate do similar things if you both won a $3 million lottery?

4 **In small groups, read about each problem. Then talk about the situation and decide what you would do.**

1. You have been offered a job that would give you three times the salary you're presently getting. The only problem is that you would have to move to a small town in a new country with a terrible climate. You're married and have two teenage children. None of you wants to move, but the high salary is very attractive. You:
a) take a chance and move.
b) stay where you are.
c) _____?_____

2. Your thirteen-year-old nephew wants to work three hours a day after school. His mother feels that he should not spend the time at a job but he should concentrate on his school work. His father disagrees. He thinks it's good for a teenager to work part time. They ask you for your opinion. You:
a) agree with his mother.
b) agree with his father.
c) _____?_____

3. Your niece is in her second year at college, and she has to decide on a major. She loves to write poetry and says that when she finishes college, she wants to write poetry full time. Her father thinks she should get a teaching degree so that she will have a more secure job after college. You:
a) agree with her father.
b) tell your niece to write full time.
c) _____?_____

continued

4. Your friend is in her late thirties. She's about to get married for the first time. She and her fiancé both have had good jobs, but she has saved money for the past fifteen years and her fiancé hasn't. She can't decide whether to keep the money she has earned in a separate account or open a joint account with her fiancé. You advise her to:
a) open a joint account.
b) keep her money in a separate account.
c) _____?_____

5 **With a partner, read the paragraph. Then write a short conversation with your partner and act it out.**

You need exact fare to get on a bus. You only have a twenty-dollar bill. The bus fare is $2.50. You ask a person who is also waiting for the bus for change. The person gives it to you.

Use the following expressions in your conversation.

Asking for change

Do you have change for a twenty?
Could you change a twenty-dollar bill?

Begin like this:

YOU: Excuse me, . . .

6 **Explain this expression.**

Money brings you food, but no appetite; medicine, but not health.

Are there any expressions about money in your culture?

Now listen as your teacher reads the following story.

Easy Come, Easy Go

Many years ago, a poor man wanted to give his king a present. The only thing the man had was a simple wooden bowl. He gave the king the bowl, and the king was very happy. The king, who lived far away and had never seen such a bowl, thought the bowl was very precious and beautiful. So pleased was he with the gift that he gave the man a pot of gold.

Now the man was richer than he ever thought possible, and he became greedy. He said to himself, "The king gave me a pot of gold for a simple wooden bowl. Imagine what the king will give me if I give him a golden chair." The man took the pot of gold and with it he bought a golden chair. When the king got the golden chair, he said, "How can I repay this man? I have only one thing that is as precious as this chair." So, the king gave the man the wooden bowl.

Do you know a similar story about money or greed?

7 Writing Suggestions

1. Write about the first time you had a job.
   a) What was it?
   b) How did you feel about it?
   c) How long did you keep it?

2. Comment on one of the following expressions:
   a) Money is the root of all evil.
   b) Don't marry for money. It's cheaper to borrow.
   c) Money can do everything.

Appendix

APPENDIX

The Appendix contains two vocabulary exercises for each chapter—a fill-in exercise and a crossword puzzle. It also contains answers to the fill-in exercises, lists of words used in each crossword puzzle and solutions to the puzzles. Teachers may use these exercises to introduce vocabulary at the start of a chapter or to review vocabulary at the end.

Here are some suggested steps to follow in completing the exercises:

1. Vocabulary fill-in exercises
   a) Each student works alone.
   b) Each student compares answers with those of a partner.
   c) The entire class goes over the answers.

2. Crossword puzzles
   a) Easy method:
      Students work in pairs. One student has the puzzle and clues; the other has the word list. They work out the puzzle together.
   b) Challenging method:
      Students work in pairs and try to complete the puzzle without looking at the word list. However, they may refer back to the appropriate chapter since every word appears there.

Nouns	Verbs	Adjectives
neighbor	complain	considerate
	disturb	hospitable
	drop in	miserable
	move	nosy
		thick

Complete the sentences using the words above. First work by yourself. Then compare your answers with those of a partner. Finally, go over them as a class.

1. The man next door is polite and friendly. I'm glad he's my _____.

2. When the baby arrives, they'll _____ to a larger apartment.

3. The fog was so _____ we could not see one foot ahead.

4. I'm fixing my kitchen sink. I hope the noise won't _____ you.

5. My boss is never satisfied. He always finds something to _____ about.

6. The Kleiners always have visitors. They're very _____.

7. Everything went wrong. The weather was bad, and the food was awful. Everyone felt _____.

8. We'll be home all evening. _____ _____ any time you want.

9. She asks many personal questions. She's very _____.

10. It was _____ of you to have helped the old man.

CROSSWORD PUZZLE 1

Across

4. opposite of *bad*
6. We live in a white _____
10. say you are sorry
11. person who lives nearby
13. I'd like to _____ you to our party.
14. Where did you and your husband first _____?
16. opposite of *sell*
17. very unhappy
18. wanting to know everyone's business
19. make believe

Down

1. Their house is always full of guests because they are so _____.
2. If he gets more money, he will _____ to a larger house.
3. He _____ thirteen years old.
5. You are always welcome. _____ in any time.
7. thoughtful of others
8. It's his. Give it to _____.
9. We built a white, wooden _____ around our house.
10. These houses _____ five years old.
11. opposite of quiet
12. He _____ the ball with the bat.
14. I wish he would _____ his own business.
15. keep money for later use

How Honest Are You?

Nouns	Verbs	Adjectives	Idiom
benefit	find	ashamed	white lie
wolf	get used to	honest	
	lie	valuable	
	steal		

Complete the sentences using the words above. First work by yourself. Then compare your answers with those of a partner. Finally, go over them as a class.

1. That ring is very _____.

2. The _____ storekeeper returned the extra dollar.

3. A long vacation is the biggest _____ of that job.

4. Don't _____ about your age. Nobody will believe you.

5. I think I left my book at your house. If you _____ it, please give it back to me tomorrow.

6. The hungry _____ ate the lamb.

7. I didn't hurt anybody when I said I was a few years younger than I am. It was a _____ _____.

8. He was _____ of the terrible way his father talked to his employees.

9. Don't leave your pocketbook on the table; someone may _____ it.

10. I can't _____ _____ _____ living without you.

CROSSWORD PUZZLE 2

Across

5. When he said I was lazy, he _____ my feelings.
6. worth a lot of money
8. At what station did he _____ on the train?
9. wild animal in the dog family
11. We plan to _____ tomatoes and cucumbers in our garden.
13. opposite of *difficult*
14. later
16. You promised to _____ the truth.
17. tell something that isn't true
18. opposite of *honest*

Down

1. He says that he didn't _____ the money. He only borrowed it.
2. You should be _____ of the mean things you said to him.
3. If you _____ on the test, the teacher will throw your test away.
4. We buy all our _____ at the supermarket.
7. He always tells the truth. He is very _____.
10. I need quarters, dimes and nickels. Do you have _____ for a dollar?
12. without having to pay
15. A small lie is a _____ lie.

What Men Look for in a Wife
What Women Look for in a Husband

Noun	Verbs	Adjectives	Adverb
suggestion	advise convince	competitive easygoing industrious neat practical talkative	slightly

Complete the sentences using the words above. First work by yourself. Then compare your answers with those of a partner. Finally, go over them as a class.

1. The baby's head feels _slightly_ warm, but I don't think she's sick.

2. The _____ man never stops working.

3. Nothing makes her angry; she's very _____ and relaxed.

4. He always wants to do better than others; he's very _____.

5. I _____ you to finish your studies before you get a job.

6. What a good _____! We're going to do just what you said.

7. Your idea is _____. It will save time and money.

8. He always has something to say. What a _____ man he is!

9. He keeps everything in order. He's very _____.

10. Everyone is trying to _____ him to stop smoking.

CROSSWORD PUZZLE 3

Across

1. He doesn't talk about himself or his feelings. He's very _____.
6. a little
7. two times
8. A _____ works in the kitchen.
9. your sister or brother's daughter
12. Everyone invites him because of his _____ personality.
14. give advice
15. Please _____ the door. I'm trying to sleep.
16. That bag is _____. It's light and has a lot of room.
17. It was so funny I couldn't stop _____.

Down

2. Children should learn to _____ money.
3. not often found
4. He's an _____ person. He never gets angry.
5. The _____ child talks to everyone she meets.
10. He won't work. He's very _____.
11. hardworking
12. persuade
13. He keeps his office _____ and tidy.

Nouns	Verbs	Adjective	Adverb	Idiom
advantage	bother	empty	alone	in favor of
cane	retire			
rule	tear			
seat				

Complete the sentences using the words above. First work by yourself. Then compare your answers with those of a partner. Finally, go over them as a class.

1. I'm busy. Please don't _____ me now.

2. The new basketball player had the _____ of being taller than the other players.

3. My uncle didn't _____ until he was seventy years old.

4. Did he _____ his shirt climbing the tree?

5. After he broke his hip, he walked with a _____.

6. She moved in with a friend because she didn't want to live _____.

7. He gave his _____ to the old woman.

8. There is a _____ against smoking in the elevator.

9. Nobody is _____ _____ _____ higher taxes.

10. Your glass is _____. Would you like some more?

CROSSWORD PUZZLE 4

Across

2. I need a new winter _____.
4. would rather
7. If you need help, just _____ for it.
12. by yourself
13. He has the _____ of being the tallest basketball player.
16. If you climb the fence, you may _____ your pants.
17. opposite of *full*
19. He's renting the house. He doesn't _____ it.
20. He wants to _____ when he is sixty-five years old.
21. I stood _____ line for an hour.
22. chair

Down

1. Since we cannot agree, let's take a _____.
3. My mother's father is my _____.
5. It is against the _____ to smoke in this room.
6. Can you do this math _____?
8. I won't _____ my son stay up after eleven.
9. How do you _____ today?
10. We are in _____ of the new plan.
11. annoy
14. At what _____ did he begin to talk?
15. They live in a _____ of people over fifty-five.
18. walking stick

5 Borrowing and Lending

Nouns	Verbs	Adjective	Adverb
interest	borrow	generous	reluctantly
mess	lend		
receipt	owe		
relative	remind		

Complete the sentences using the words above. First work by yourself. Then compare your answers with those of a partner. Finally, go over them as a class.

1. It's very _____ of you to give her so much money.

2. I still _____ the bank five thousand dollars.

3. He didn't want to sell his house. He _____ sold it.

4. You dropped the food; now clean up the _____.

5. Would you _____ me your watch just for today?

6. When you buy an expensive item, you should keep your _____.

7. If you get ten percent _____ on $1,000, you will have $1,100 in one year.

8. I don't want to _____ his old car. It's too dangerous to drive.

9. If I don't _____ him, he'll forget.

10. He's my _____ through marriage.

CROSSWORD PUZZLE 5

Across

1. That restaurant was expensive. The _____ came to over $200.
3. The _____ man gave gifts to all the children in the hospital.
5. opposite of *near*
7. If you want to return anything in this store, you need your _____.
8. What is your _____ toward money?
11. He never puts anything away. His house is a big _____.
13. How much did you _____ for your watch?
14. I borrowed $50. I paid back $20. I _____ $30.
16. In my _____, it isn't a good idea.
17. I forgot my money. Would you _____ me a dollar?

Down

1. I must _____ money from the bank in order to start a business.
2. I put my money in this bank because it pays a high rate of _____.
4. Who will take _____ of your dog when you are away?
6. destroy
7. Doesn't he _____ you of that actor?
9. She can't reach the button. It's _____ high for her.
10. Would you do me a _____ and help me carry these books?
12. a husband or wife
15. Do you have an _____ for coming late?

Nouns	Verbs	Adjectives
raise	blush	due
weight	earn	embarrassing
	gain	impolite
	vote	pregnant

Complete the sentences using the words above. First work by yourself. Then compare your answers with those of a partner. Finally, go over them as a class.

1. Did he _____ when that beautiful girl spoke to him?

2. She gave the _____ woman a seat.

3. They don't know how to behave. They're very _____.

4. The rent is _____ on the first of the month.

5. He ate a lot, but he didn't _____ a pound.

6. We usually _____ for a class president at the beginning of the school year.

7. When did he _____ so much money?

8. She turned red when he asked that _____ question.

9. He put on a lot of _____ after he retired.

10. If you continue to do such good work, you will get a _____.

CROSSWORD PUZZLE 6

Across

2. He only works _____ time.
4. You are _____. I'm not that actress.
5. brother's or sister's son
7. I've read this book ten times. It's my _____ book.
11. This bill is _____ on October 30.
12. Nobody under eighteen years can _____ in this election.
13. A person between forty and sixty is _____-aged.
14. I _____ when he said all those nice things about me.
17. Did the sun _____ behind a cloud?
18. The _____ of *hot* is *cold*.
19. I ate so much on my vacation that I _____ five pounds.

Down

1. His work was so good that he got a big _____.
2. expecting a baby
3. How much money does he _____ in a year?
6. After many unhappy years together, they _____ divorced.
8. Please _____ me. I didn't mean to push you.
9. He isn't short or tall. He's _____ height.
10. Don't kiss your teenage son in public. You are _____ him.
15. His death came as a great _____ to all of us.
16. rude

Dress for Success

Nouns	Verbs	Adjectives
style	avoid	concerned
suit	judge	tight
uniform	prevent	
	sew	
	wrap	

Complete the sentences using the words above. First work by yourself. Then compare your answers with those of a partner. Finally, go over them as a class.

1. I can't wear those shoes. They're too _____.

2. The school principal is _____ about the boy's poor work.

3. At his other job he wore jeans. For this one he wears a _____ and tie.

4. Every policeman wore a blue _____.

5. We will try to _____ making the same mistake twice.

6. You must pay extra if you want someone to _____ the gift.

7. He learned to _____ in the army, and so his children come to him when their clothes are torn.

8. That magazine says that long hair is not in _____ this season.

9. Can you _____ which story is better?

10. Did his low grades in math and science _____ him from getting into that college?

CROSSWORD PUZZLE 7

Across

2. In my _____, clothes are not important.
5. Does the soup _____ too salty?
6. He usually wears a _____ and tie to work.
7. Don't forget to _____ the present.
9. opposite of *most*
12. He always wears a dark suit and tie. He dresses in a _____ way.
15. Lower the _____ and it will be easy to sell.
16. What is the latest _____ in women's clothes?

Down

1. He _____ his leg when he fell.
3. I'm wearing a new dress for the job _____.
4. I lost a _____ from my jacket.
8. How can we _____ the spread of the disease?
10. He needs to _____ a button on his shirt.
11. Let's leave early to _____ traffic.
12. The _____ of the book is red and black.
13. opposite of *loose*
14. opposite of *expensive*

8   **Giving the Right Gift**

Nouns	Verb	Adjective	Adverb
cologne equipment gift hint jewelry occasion scent	feed	formal	approximately

Complete the sentences using the words above. First work alone. Then compare your answers with those of a partner. Finally, go over them as a class.

1. He usually gives his wife a piece of _____ on her birthday.

2. His arms were so weak the nurse had to _____ him.

3. The school bought new _____ for the science laboratory.

4. You can smell her coming. She always wears a lot of _____.

5. Those roses have a wonderful _____.

6. You can't wear jeans to a _____ dinner party.

7. It takes _____ five hours to fly from New York to Los Angeles.

8. It's my nephew's first birthday. I'm looking for a special _____.

9. Give me a _____ about what you want for your birthday.

10. On what _____ do people in the United States eat turkey and sweet potatoes?

CROSSWORD PUZZLE 8

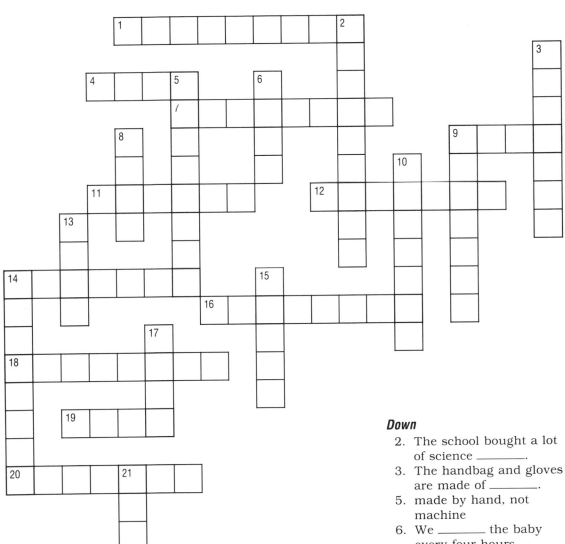

Across

1. opposite of *cheap*
4. having a lot of money
7. He is sneezing because he is _____ to the fur of cats.
9. How much did it _____?
11. They wore _____ clothes to the dinner party.
12. bracelets, rings, necklaces, etc.
14. Her boyfriend gave her a bottle of _____ for her birthday.
16. choice
18. It was a _____ to see him again.
19. a small or indirect suggestion
20. She is _____ to me through marriage.

Down

2. The school bought a lot of science _____.
3. The handbag and gloves are made of _____.
5. made by hand, not machine
6. We _____ the baby every four hours.
8. having very little money
9. sure
10. When we get married, we will have a big _____.
13. She doesn't have brothers or sisters. She's an _____ child.
14. think about
15. I love the _____ of your perfume.
17. present
21. object for a child to play with

87

Nouns	Verbs	Adjective
choice	join	athletic
coach	kick	
score	miss	
sport	narrow	
team		

Complete the sentences using the words above. First work alone. Then compare your answers with those of a partner. Finally, go over them as a class.

1. He became a _____ of his son's Little League team.

2. I just came to this game. What's the _____?

3. Many of the girls on the volleyball _____ are better than the boys.

4. Did the ball hit the window or _____ it?

5. She is both intelligent and _____.

6. Anyone can _____ this baseball team. You don't have to be a good baseball player.

7. Football can be a dangerous _____.

8. He hurt his foot, so he can't _____ well.

9. We will _____ the choices down to two possibilities.

10. I agree with your decision. You made a good _____.

CROSSWORD PUZZLE 9

Across

2. Marks you get for schoolwork are called _____.
5. He chose five, but he must _____ down his choices to three.
6. Many children join _____ League teams.
8. opposite of *fat*
10. We don't know who's winning because we aren't keeping _____.
11. My favorite _____ is soccer.
12. take it easy
14. quick at learning
15. hit with the foot
16. a group that works or plays together

Down

1. one you like most
2. You get a point in soccer when the ball goes in the other team's _____.
3. It is never nice to _____ fun of others.
4. a person who leads and works with a sports team
7. well-liked
9. She plans to _____ a woman's basketball team next fall.
10. The best players are on an All-_____ team.
13. When he picked that car, he made a good _____.

Nouns	Adjectives	Idiom
experiment	allowed	no wonder
lawn	mean	
pet	stubborn	
	terrible	
	terrific	
	wise	

Complete the sentences using the words above. First work by yourself. Then compare your answers with those of a partner. Finally, go over them as a class.

1. Many people think a dog is a good _____.

2. Be careful! That dog is very _____.

3. They asked the _____ old man for advice.

4. He is so _____. He will never change his mind.

5. You have been running for a long time. _____ _____ you're tired!

6. It was such a _____ movie that many people left before it was over.

7. Don't sit on the _____. It's wet.

8. Everyone enjoyed the show. The actors and actresses did a _____ job.

9. The animal died after the scientist performed her _____.

10. You are not _____ to smoke in this classroom.

CROSSWORD PUZZLE 10

Across

2. He caught a big _____ in the pond.
5. animal you keep in your home
6. Who is in _____ of higher taxes?
8. They fell _____ love and got married soon after.
9. I _____ my bird every day.
10. an animal with long ears and a round tail
13. Our dog likes to _____ a hole in our backyard.
14. The sign says, "_____ of dog."
16. The grass is beautiful on their front _____.
17. opposite of *pretty*
18. illness
19. very good
21. I won't rent the apartment because pets are not _____.

Down

1. Business was so good they were able to _____ three more people.
3. There's a big _____ in my sock.
4. He left because he can't _____ the smell of cooked broccoli.
5. opposite of *public*
7. very bad
11. unkind
12. You went to bed late. No _____ you are so tired.
15. He died without leaving a _____.
20. Scientists are trying to find a _____ for that sickness.

Nouns	Verbs	Adjectives
advertisements	force	overweight
alcoholic	notice	local
cancer	reach	
supervisor	refuse	

Complete the sentences using the words above. First work by yourself. Then compare your answers with those of a partner. Finally, go over them as a class.

1. If you _____ to work late, you will lose your job.

2. The doctor said that few people die of that form of _____.

3. There are many _____ for cars in the newspaper on Thursday.

4. Our _____ newspaper won two prizes for good reporting.

5. The doctor said he is twenty pounds _____.

6. My _____ helps anyone who has a problem at work.

7. The baby can't _____ the top shelf.

8. I _____ women are wearing both short and long skirts.

9. The police officer will _____ him to leave if he continues to make so much noise.

10. He used to be an _____, but he stopped drinking when he started a new job.

Across

1. You don't have to go far. The _____ library has everything you need.
5. Put out your cigarette. The sign says, "No _____."
8. He has _____ of the throat.
9. person in charge
12. go away
13. I'm _____ working on the same puzzle. It's very difficult.
14. It is _____ to give him all the work.
19. The _____ is that the winner keeps the money.
20. weighing more than you should
21. Don't _____ the child to eat. He'll eat when he's hungry.
23. She was wearing a new dress, but he didn't even _____.

Down

2. His _____ are black from smoking too much.
3. I will _____ his present under the bed.
4. Smoking is a bad _____.
5. I can _____ that the milk isn't fresh.
6. The doctor is ready for the next _____.
7. I'm trying to _____ him to buy a new car.
10. Every afternoon the children play in the _____.
11. I'm too short. I can't _____ the top shelf.
15. person who drinks too much alcohol
16. He is trying to _____ up smoking.
17. They always fight. They can't _____ on anything.
18. They _____ against the high price of milk.
22. twenty plus twenty

Nouns	Verbs	Adjectives
allowance	concentrate	exact
climate	drop out	precious
major	graduate	
majority		
salary		

Complete the sentences using the words above. First work by yourself. Then compare your answers with those of a partner. Finally, go over them as a class.

1. What will you do when you _____ from college?

2. That picture of her grandmother is _____ to her.

3. There is so much noise it is hard to _____.

4. His _____ is low but he enjoys his work.

5. His father gave him a ten-dollar _____ every week.

6. He wants to _____ _____ of school and get a job.

7. He plans to be a chemistry _____ in college.

8. The _____ of people are for him.

9. It never gets very hot or very cold. San Francisco has a mild _____.

10. I need to know the _____ spelling of your name.

Across

2. That toy bear is John's most _____ possession.
6. I know the store is nearby, but I don't know the _____ address.
7. It's _____. All the strong players are on one team.
10. His father gave him a five-dollar _____ every week.
14. Don't drop _____ of school. You won't be able to find a good job.
16. opposite of *expensive*
17. It will _____ you $100 to fly to Miami from New York.
18. He has a _____ job, but it isn't very interesting.
19. His _____ requires a lot of travel.
21. Everyone was afraid to buy that land. He took a _____ and became rich.
22. Let's get to the _____ of the problem.
23. He won a million dollars in the _____.

Down

1. We both own the house. We are _____ owners.
3. The bus _____ is $1.
4. How much did you _____ for your notebook?
5. He will _____ from high school next June.
8. Many people _____ to Florida when they retire.
9. She doesn't _____ much money, but she enjoys her work.
11. I'm so excited, I can't _____.
12. He eats a lot. He has a big _____.
13. His parents _____ him to study hard.
15. I have a savings _____ at two banks.
20. He won't take that job because the _____ is too low.

Answers to Fill-in Exercises

1
1. neighbor
2. move
3. thick
4. disturb
5. complain
6. hospitable
7. miserable
8. Drop in
9. nosy
10. considerate

2
1. valuable
2. honest
3. benefit
4. lie
5. find
6. wolf
7. white lie
8. ashamed
9. steal
10. get used to

3
1. slightly
2. industrious
3. easygoing
4. competitive
5. advise
6. suggestion
7. practical
8. talkative
9. neat
10. convince

4
1. bother
2. advantage
3. retire
4. tear
5. cane
6. alone
7. seat
8. rule
9. in favor of
10. empty

5
1. generous
2. owe
3. reluctantly
4. mess
5. lend
6. receipt
7. interest
8. borrow
9. remind
10. relative

6
1. blush
2. pregnant
3. impolite
4. due
5. gain
6. vote
7. earn
8. embarrassing
9. weight
10. raise

7
1. tight
2. concerned
3. suit
4. uniform
5. avoid
6. wrap
7. sew
8. style
9. judge
10. prevent

8
1. jewelry
2. feed
3. equipment
4. cologne
5. scent
6. formal
7. approximately
8. gift
9. hint
10. occasion

9
1. coach
2. score
3. team
4. miss
5. athletic
6. join
7. sport
8. kick
9. narrow
10. choice

10
1. pet
2. mean
3. wise
4. stubborn
5. No wonder
6. terrible
7. lawn
8. terrific
9. experiment
10. allowed

11
1. refuse
2. cancer
3. advertisements
4. local
5. overweight
6. supervisor
7. reach
8. notice
9. force
10. alcoholic

12
1. graduate
2. precious
3. concentrate
4. salary
5. allowance
6. drop out
7. major
8. majority
9. climate
10. exact

Word Lists for Crossword Puzzles

1 You and Your Neighbors

apologize	good	is	neighbor
are	him	meet	noisy
buy	hit	mind	nosy
considerate	hospitable	miserable	pretend
drop	house	move	save
fence	invite		

2 How Honest Are You?

afterwards	easy	honest	tell
ashamed	free	hurt	valuable
change	get	lie	white
cheat	groceries	steal	wolf
dishonest	grow		

3 What Men Look for in a Wife
What Women Look for in a Husband

advise	industrious	outgoing	save
charming	laughing	practical	shut
convince	lazy	rare	slightly
cook	neat	reserved	twice
easygoing	niece		

4 The Golden Years

advantage	coat	in	retire
age	community	let	rules
alone	empty	own	seat
ask	favor	prefer	tear
bother	feel	problem	vote
cane	grandfather		

97

5   Borrowing and Lending

attitude	far	mess	remind
bill	favor	opinion	ruin
borrow	generous	owe	spouse
care	interest	pay	too
excuse	lend	receipt	

6   Red Faces

average	embarrassing	impolite	part
blushed	excuse	middle	pregnant
disappear	favorite	mistaken	raise
due	gained	nephew	shock
earn	got	opposite	vote

7   Dress for Success

avoid	hurt	prevent	suit
button	interview	price	taste
cheap	least	sew	tight
conservative	opinion	style	wrap
cover			

8   Giving the Right Gift

allergic	equipment	hint	rich
certain	expensive	jewelry	scent
cologne	feed	leather	surprise
consider	formal	only	toy
cost	gift	poor	wedding
decision	handmade	related	

9 Sports

bright	grades	narrow	sport
choice	join	popular	star
coach	kick	relax	team
favorite	little	score	thin
goal	make		

10 Pets

allowed	feed	mean	terrible
beware	fish	pet	terrific
cure	hire	private	ugly
dig	hole	rabbit	will
disease	in	stand	wonder
favor	lawn		

11 No Smoking Allowed

agree	give	notice	rule
alcoholic	habit	overweight	smell
cancer	hide	park	smoking
convince	leave	patient	still
force	local	protested	supervisor
forty	lungs	reach	unfair

12 Money

account	cost	job	precious
allowance	earn	joint	root
appetite	encourage	lottery	salary
chance	exact	move	secure
cheap	fare	out	unfair
concentrate	graduate	pay	

Solutions to Crossword Puzzles

CROSSWORD PUZZLE 1

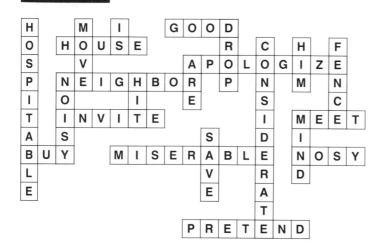

CROSSWORD PUZZLE 2

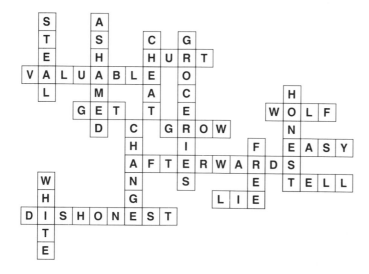

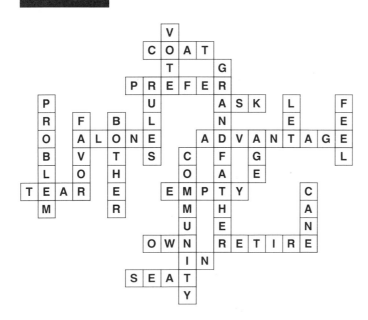

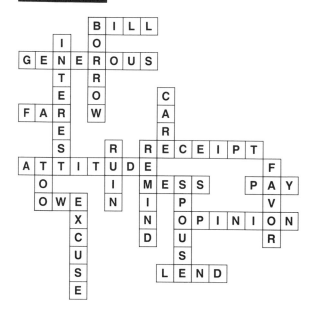

CROSSWORD PUZZLE 7

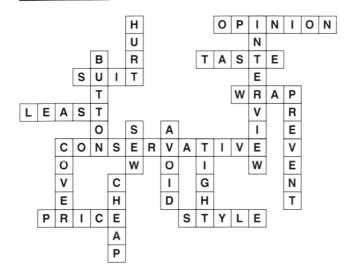

CROSSWORD PUZZLE 8

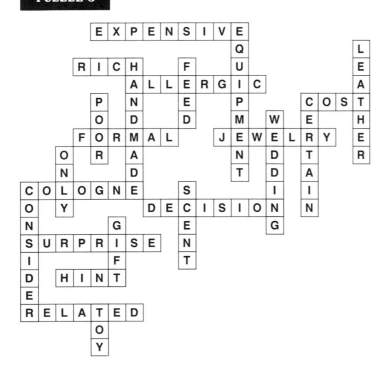

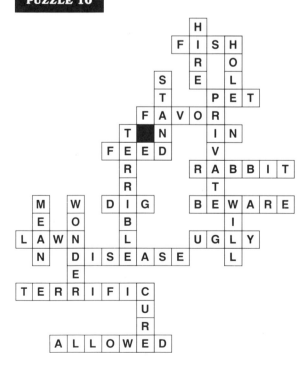

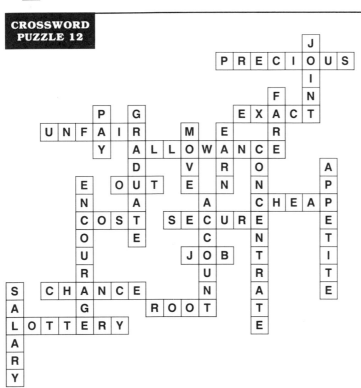